Celebrating a Life, Mourning a Death

A Guide for Professional & Informal Funeral Celebrants

Trevor Donnelly

Copyright © 2019 Trevor Donnelly
All rights reserved.
ISBN: 9781073323159
Imprint: Independently published

DEDICATION

To all those who I have loved,
but see no longer.

CONTENTS

	Acknowledgments	iv
1	Who is this Book For?	1
2	Funerals Step-by-Step	4
3	A Secular Service	8
4	Readings and Resources	33
5	Readings with Faith	45
6	Bible Readings	52
7	Writing a Eulogy	60
8	Symbolic Acts	63
9	Celebrating or Mourning	68
10	About the Author	70

ACKNOWLEDGMENTS

With Thanks

This book is the result of over 20 years of taking funerals. I owe a huge debt of gratitude to all those who have helped shaped my practice over the years, starting with the Reverend Dr David Hoyle, who trained me in the art of funerals from a Church of England perspective, and continuing through time in the Funeral Industry with with colleagues such as Philip Smyth, Brian Parsons and Valerie Orpen. Over the years my funerals have become less and less religious, the focus shifting from 'the hope of resurrection' to 'celebrating the life' of the deceased and giving their loved ones a chance to publicly mourn their passing. After years of drift, I finally jumped ship and became a secular celebrant.

Every funeral I have taken over the years has taught me something. So thank you to the many hundreds (by now over a thousand) of families and friends who granted me the privilege of taking the funeral of their loved one.

A word on Copyright:

All the readings in this book are from sources that are out of copyright. I prefer to use "old words" in my services as they give the service a certain *gravitas*. I also feel that there is comfort to be had in knowing that our struggle with mortality is an ancient one, that has perplexed humanity for countless generations.

The other words in this book, the words of the service itself are largely my own. However, 'nothing is new under the sun' and I am sure the text is a mixture of my originality alongside half-remembered words from funerals I have attended and quotes bubbling up from my subconscious. If I have breached your copyright please accept my apologies and let me know so that I can either delete or attribute in future editions.

1 WHO IS THIS BOOK FOR?

I wrote this book for myself. As I started to work as a funeral celebrant I gathered resources for *my own* practice.

A religious celebrant can simply find the relevant liturgy book and and most of the words are given to them. The Reflection / Eulogy (also known as the "Sermon") is the only bit that changes each time in a religious service.

For the secular celebrant, *every word* of the funeral can be personalised. This is possible because the focus of the secular funeral is not on God or a hope for life-after-death, but rather the focus is *entirely* on the deceased and the memories of those left behind. However, there are still words that can be used time and again: there are only so many ways to say 'welcome' or to introduce a reading. With this in mind I decided a 'book of words' would be helpful.

However, a secular service book will require many options and vast flexibility. I could not find anything like this currently on the market, so I decided to write one!

My primary audience is me, but it may also help anyone else in a similar situation.

I don't have enough faith to work as a Priest or Minister (although once upon a time I did), and I don't have enough atheism to buy into the British Humanist Society. I have great respect for both, and this book may be useful to religious and non-religious celebrants, but I fall in between the two. I suspect that is where most people are, most of the time.

I believe this book could also be of use to families putting together a service without an outside celebrant. This book will give you enough information to run a service yourself without celebrant or clergy. I believe that *anyone* with some confidence in public speaking could lead a funeral or memorial service.

The role of the celebrant can vary from "the person who does *all* the speaking," to a "master of ceremonies," who introduces a series of Tributes, Readings and Music but says very little aside from introductions. Usually the celebrant's role will be somewhere in between the two.

If you are new to being a celebrant, you may think that acting as 'master of ceremonies' is the easiest option, however, in my experience the reverse is true. As a master of ceremonies you do not have control over what people are going to say and, more importantly, how long they will take to say it. If the nephew's Tribute that you had planned to be the 'heart and soul' of the service is thirty seconds of inaudible sobs you can be left with time to fill and nothing prepared to fill it! Conversely, if they talk too long you may end up having to cut short later aspects of the service. It is vitally important to gently warn families that this could happen - be sensitive, but warn them more than once (at the time of meeting them and later as you run through the order of service). Telling the family is important as it will focus their mind when preparing their contributions and it will manage their expectations.

2 A FUNERAL STEP-BY-STEP

This is a suggested shape of a funeral service. It provides a basic order that can be filled with material personal to the deceased.
Some items are marked as "optional," but in reality *everything* is optional and can be rearranged, removed or added to according to the needs of the mourners.

Opening Music (optional):

Music is played while the guests take their seats before the service. Typically this will be faded out before the funeral begins.
Most crematoriums have the capacity to play music, either from an online system or C.D.s. (Be careful with C.D.s - many chapels will not accept home-copied C.D.s - only original disks.) Also, crematorium chapels usually have an organ (although some charge an extra fee for an organist).
Cemetery chapels do not usually have these facilities, some do not even have electricity.

Welcome:

This is usually the celebrant's job. They welcome the guests and introduce the service.

First Hymn/Song/Music (optional):

Traditionally hymns would be sung at a funeral. These days playing a song or a piece of music that the deceased enjoyed is increasingly common. Usually the music would be faded out after a verse or two.

Reading (optional):

There may be one or more readings of poetry or prose. These can be read by either the celebrant or one of the mourners.

Tribute(s):

Either a family member or friend will say a few words or the celebrant will read information about the life of the deceased that they have organised with the family and/or friends. If the celebrant is reading this, it will usually merge with the next section: the Reflection / Eulogy...

Reflection / Eulogy:

The celebrant or a mourner may give a brief reflection on life and death.

Committal:

The moment of goodbye. In the crematorium the curtains may close, there may be silence or a prayer. You may prefer to leave the curtain open and say goodbye as you leave the Crematorium.

Second Hymn/Song/Music (optional):

As before, usually the music would be faded out after a verse or two.

End of Service:

Some concluding words or a prayer for a blessing may be said.

Closing Music (optional):

Some music may be played as the guests leave the Chapel.

* * *

A note about timings

Time slots in the crematorium vary from 20 to 60 minutes. You can book a double slot (if you are prepared to pay the extra fee). It is part of the celebrant's job to make sure the service keeps to time. The celebrant will make sure the service is planned to fit in the allotted time, however, if a tribute over-runs the celebrant may have to shorten music or cut out some later parts of the service.

3 SECULAR FUNERAL SERVICE

This is designed to be a liturgy book for secular services (see 'The Book of Common Prayer' or 'Common Worship' to see the religious equivalent).

There are blank spaces left where you can stick a Post-It note with the details of your service (the name of the artist and song for music or the details of who is delivering the Tribute.
I also place Post-Its to cover options that you will not be using (like the possible prayers if you are taking a service for a passionate atheist).

I prefer to have every word I'm going to say written out in full, it stops me 'waffling' and keeps me focused. You may find it unnatural to use someone else's words and want to personalise it to fit your style.

ORDER OF SERVICE

[*The celebrant walks in ahead of the coffin as the opening music plays.*]

Opening Music:

***

Welcome:

Today we have gathered here to pay our last respects and to say our final farewells to **Name**; to pay tribute to **his/her** life, and to express our love and admiration for **him/her**. Also, we gather to show our support and to bring comfort to those of **his/her** family and friends who are here in the depths of grief.

[*Especially if there is division in the family/ friends:*]

We have come together from different places;

we are all at different stages on our journey through life; our paths are varied; we look at life in different ways. But there is one thing we all have in common,
at one point or another, our lives have been touched by, and have touched, the life of **Name**.

And so this **afternoon** we've put aside our usual daily round for a while, and gathered here to give expression to the thoughts and feelings that well up in us at this time of loss.

[*In Tragic Circumstances:*]

We gather here to mark the tragic passing of **Name**. We may feel shock, or despair or we may be numbed by *the events that took **him/her** from us*. But this time can be transformed by love, and by remembering all that **Name** was to us, and all that **his/her** memories will continue to be.

***

Hymn/Song/Music:

***

Reading:

[*If there are printed Orders of Service:*]

Please but down your Orders of Service for a moment and listen to **Reader's Name** as ***he/she*** reads for us...

***

Family Tribute(s):

***

End of Tributes:

Hold on to some of these memories now as we spend a few moments in silence and you can each remember **Name** in your own way, and those of you that do have a religious faith might like to use this time for your own private prayer.

***

Reflection / Eulogy:

I have been asked to say a few words.
This is a difficult day. Facing up to the loss of those we love is the hardest thing we ever have to do. We may be saddened to a point where words cannot describe our sadness.

We may feel that it is over. **Name** is lost to us, and **his/her** story is at an end.

We are gathered here to remember. At this moment our thoughts may now be filled with **Name**'s last days and weeks, **his/her** *failing health...*

...but also, if we are to truly honour **Name**'s life, we must remember back further, to all that **he/she** was, and all **he/she** was to us...

- *a loving husband/wife/partner to ...,*
- *a proud father/mother to...,*
- *a doting grandfather/grandmother to...,*
- *to all of us a friend or neighbour...*

Name may be taken from us, but **he/she** lives on in the memories of all who knew **him/her**, this is *not* the end. As we recall ***his/her*** life we can get to know ***him/her*** better. ***His/Her*** story is not over, and ***his/her*** part in your story is not over either. Remember all that ***he/she*** gave you, and remember that you gave ***him/her*** joy too. As you remember, realise that you are not done with **Name** and **Name** is not done with you.

Sadly I did not have the privilege if meeting **Name** during ***his/her*** life, but you will have many memories.

[If this is also the Tribute, insert the life story here...]

***

[*After a long illness (especially of the deceased was a music lover):*]

The opposite of music is not silence. In many great pieces of music their are pauses and silences that make the music more beautiful or striking. The opposite of music is not silence it is discord. The discord of **Name**'s long illness is over, and now there is, at least to our ears, silence. Death is not the end of life, but merely a part of the music of its endless round. We mourn because **Name** is gone from us. **He/She** no longer with us in the flesh. However, we are left with the faith that **Name** may gone from our sight but **he/she** is not gone from our hearts and thoughts and memories.

[*If the deceased had a partner:*]

Those nearest to **Name** will *always* miss **him/her** but our pain becomes part of our life, as life does go on. Our pain is mixed with joy as we remember all the good times of the past. We get used to our grief, like getting used to wearing a wedding ring. It becomes a part of us.

[*Former teachers / mentors:*]

I am reminded of *Epitaph On A Friend* by Robert Burns

An honest man here lies at rest,
The friend of man, the friend of truth,
The friend of age, and guide of youth:
Few hearts like his, with virtue warm'd,
Few heads with knowledge so inform'd;
If there's another world, he lives in bliss;
If there is none, he made the best of this.

[*SciFi Nerds / Science Geeks:*]

Name enjoyed science **fiction** and looked to the stars. Stars are fascinating because they burn with the heat of a nuclear reaction. They shine because they *burn*. So the process by which they die is the same as the process by which they live. A star cannot be a star unless one day it dies. And so it is for us, and so it has been for **Name**. **He/She** shone **his/her** light into our lives, and now **he/she** is gone. But the universe has forever been changed, forever made brighter by **Name**'s time in it.

[*Or...*]

After the Big Bang, scientists believe that the only elements that existed were hydrogen and helium (the lightest and simplest elements). No carbon or metal or any complex elements. Then these atoms of hydrogen and helium slowly clustered over unimaginable aeons of time the clusters became enormous balls of matter that had so much gravity that the atoms were pulled apart in a nuclear reaction, and the universe's first generation of stars sprung to light.

All of the heavy elements that exist in the universe – metals, and the carbon of our bodies, were created in the heart of the first generation of stars. Our human bodies that we so often feel ashamed of (or are frustrated by) are the stuff of stars, made in depths of space, at the heart of the mystery of the universe. Life is short and contains sad days like today, but life is also wonderful and beautiful, and as we remember the life of **Name** we can see wonder and beauty in the time we shared with ***him/her***.

[*A good ending to the Eulogy, especially if it is quite short:*]

I close this part of the service with the poem ***He/She*** Is Gone, by David Harkins:

You can shed tears that **he** is gone
Or you can smile because he has lived
You can close your eyes
  and pray that he will come back
Or you can open your eyes
  and see all that he has left
Your heart can be empty
  because you can't see him
Or you can be full
  of the love that you shared
You can turn your back on tomorrow
  and live yesterday
Or you can be happy for tomorrow
  because of yesterday
You can remember him
  and only that he is gone
Or you can cherish his memory
  and let it live on
You can cry and close your mind,
  be empty and turn your back
Or you can do what he would want:
      smile, open your eyes, love and go on

[*Or...*]

You can shed tears that **she** is gone
Or you can smile because she has lived
You can close your eyes
   and pray that she will come back
Or you can open your eyes
   and see all that she has left
Your heart can be empty
   because you can't see her
Or you can be full
   of the love that you shared
You can turn your back on tomorrow
   and live yesterday
Or you can be happy for tomorrow
   because of yesterday
You can remember her
   and only that she is gone
Or you can cherish her memory
   and let it live on
You can cry and close your mind,
   be empty and turn your back
Or you can do what she would want:
      smile, open your eyes, love and go on.

***

Committal:

Please stand.

As **Name**'s body will cremated, and **his/her** ashes returned to the earth, **he/she** will *become* the earth, like a drop of water retuning to the ocean.
Although **Name** will see no more sunrises, walk in no more woods, feel no more the rain on **his/her** face; **Name** will *become* the sunrise, *become* the woods and become the rain.

[*And/or:*]

Please stand.

We now mark the end of the physical existence of **Name**. And we say goodbye. He will live now in our memories,
may those memories bring us comfort in the sadness of this goodbye.

[*Or:*]

Please stand.

Over two thousand years ago, an unknown scribe wrote,
"To everything there is a season,
and a time to every purpose under heaven,
...a time to dance and a time to mourn...
a time to be born and a time to die..."

[*Or:*]

Please stand.

In the words of Samuel Butler:
"I fall asleep in the full and certain hope
That my slumber shall not be broken;
And that though I be all-forgetting,
Yet shall I not be forgotten.
But continue that life
in the thoughts and deeds
Of those I loved."

[*Or:*]

Please stand.

In the words of John Dryden:
"Like pilgrims
  to the appointed place we tend;
The world's an inn,
  and death the journey's end."

[*Or:*]

Please stand.

In the words of the Buddha:
"The way is not the sky.
The way is in the heart."

***

[If there was no silence earlier in the service:]

We now spend a few moments in silence and you can each remember **Name** in your own way, and those of you that do have a religious faith might like to use this time for your own private prayer.

***

Hymn/Song/Music:

***

Prayers:

[If the family want some religion....:]

Eternal God,
in your hands are the souls of the living
and the spirits of all creatures.
We turn to you in grief as well as in joy,
for your mercy is always with us,
and your love and truth support us at all times.
Though we walk through the valley
of the shadow of death,
we fear no harm,
for you are beside us;
your rod and staff they comfort us.
Lord, you have taken from us **Name**.
In your mercy bear **her/him** to life everlasting.
May the memory of **her/his** life
and **her/his** good deeds
bring blessing and comfort
to those who mourn for **her/him**.
May it give them the courage and strength
to continue bravely in their daily life,
trusting you in their hearts.
God of mercy, help those who mourn,
and comfort them in their grief.
Lighten their darkness,

and console them in their sorrow.
It is said: "As a mother comforts her child
so will I myself comfort you.
Never again shall your sun set,
nor your moon withdraw its light,
because the Lord will be your everlasting light,
and the days of your mourning will be ended."
Amen.

***

The Lord's Prayer:

Our Father, who art in heaven,
hallowed be thy name;
thy kingdom come; thy will be done;
on earth as it is in heaven.
Give us this day our daily bread.
And forgive us our trespasses,
as we forgive
those who trespass against us.
And lead us not into temptation;
but deliver us from evil.
For thine is the kingdom,
the power and the glory,
for ever and ever. Amen.

***

Support us, O Lord,
all the day long of this troublous life,
until the shadows lengthen
and the evening comes,
the busy world is hushed,
the fever of life is over
and our work is done.
Then, Lord, in your mercy
grant us a safe lodging,
a holy rest,
and peace at the last;
through Christ our Lord.
Amen.

***

Hymn/Song/Music:

***

End of Service:

Our time together here is almost at an end, but before we part lets remind ourselves that ***Name*** does not reside in a coffin or an urn, but in the hearts and minds of the lives that **he/she** touched.

[Information about the wake & closing music...]

[*End with one of these, or another poem (unless there has already been a lot of poetry):*]

We have come to the end of this ceremony for **Name**, I will give the last words to Christina Rossetti's poem, "Let Me Go:"

When I come to the end of the road
And the sun has set for me
I want no rites in a gloom filled room
Why cry for a soul set free?
Miss me a little, but not for long
And not with your head bowed low
Remember the love that once we shared
Miss me, but let me go.
For this is a journey we all must take
And each must go alone.
It's all part of the master plan
A step on the road to home.
When you are lonely and sick at heart
Go to the friends we know.
Laugh at all the things we used to do
Miss me, but let me go.

[*Or:*]

We have come to the end of this ceremony for **Name**, I will give the last words to Winston Churchill:

Let us be contented with what has happened and be thankful for all that we have been spared. Let us accept the natural order of things in which we move.
Let us reconcile ourselves to the mysterious rhythm of our destinies, such as they must be in this world of space and time.
Let us treasure our joys but not bewail our sorrows. The glory of light cannot exist without its shadows.
Life is a whole, and good and ill must be accepted together. The journey has been enjoyable and well worth making - once.

***

Closing Music:

***

4 READINGS & RESOURCES

Let Me Go by Christina Rossetti,

When I come to the end of the road
And the sun has set for me
I want no rites in a gloom filled room
Why cry for a soul set free?
Miss me a little, but not for long
And not with your head bowed low
Remember the love that once we shared
Miss me, but let me go.
For this is a journey we all must take
And each must go alone.
It's all part of the master plan
A step on the road to home.
When you are lonely and sick at heart
Go to the friends we know.
Laugh at all the things we used to do
Miss me, but let me go.

Do Not Stand At My Grave and Weep
by Mary Frye

Do not stand at my grave and weep
I am not there.
I do not sleep.
I am a thousand winds that blow.
I am the diamond glints on snow.
I am the sunlight on ripened grain.
I am the gentle autumn's rain.
When you awaken in the morning's hush,
I am the swift uplifting rush
Of quiet birds in circled flight.
I am the soft stars that shine at night.
Do not stand at my grave and cry;
I am not there.
I did not die.

If I should die before the rest of you
by Joyce Grenfell

If I should die before the rest of you
Break not a flower nor inscribe a stone
Nor, when I'm gone, speak in a Sunday voice,
But be the usual selves that I have known.
Weep if you must
Parting is hell.
But life goes on.
So sing as well.

Instructions by Arnold Crompton

When I have moved beyond you
  in the adventure of life,
Gather in some pleasant place
  and there remember me
With spoken words, old and new.
Let a tear if you will, but let a smile come quickly
For I have loved the laughter of life.
Do not linger too long with your solemnities.
Go eat and talk, and when you can;
Follow a woodland trail, climb a high mountain,
Walk along the wild seashore,
Chew the thoughts of some book
Which challenges your soul.
Use your hands some bright day
To make a thing of beauty
Or to lift someone's heavy load.
Though you mention not my name,
Though no thought of me crosses your mind,
I shall be with you,
For these have been the realities
  of my life for me.
And when you face some crisis with anguish.
When you walk alone with courage,
When you choose your path of right,
I shall be very close to you.
I have followed the valleys,
I have climbed the heights of life.

Not, how did he die, but how did he live?
Anonymous

Not, how did he die, but how did he live?
Not, what did he gain, but what did he give?
These are the units to measure the worth
Of a man as a man, regardless of his birth.
Nor what was his church, nor what was his creed?
But had he befriended those really in need?
Was he ever ready, with words of good cheer,
To bring back a smile, to banish a tear?
Not what did the sketch in the newspaper say,
But how many were sorry when he passed away?

Afterglow by Helen Lowrie Marshall

I'd like the memory of me to be a happy one.
I'd like to leave an afterglow
  of smiles when life is done.
I'd like to leave an echo
  whispering softly down the ways,
Of happy times and laughing times
  and bright and sunny days.
I'd like the tears of those who grieve,
  to dry before the sun;
Of happy memories that I leave
  when life is done.

We Remember Him (We Remember Her)
adapted from the Yizkor Service

When we are weary and in need of strength,
When we are lost and sick at heart,
We remember him.
When we have a joy we crave to share
When we have decisions that are difficult to make
When we have achievements that are based on his
We remember him.
At the blowing of the wind
and in the chill of winter
At the opening of the buds
and in the rebirth of spring,
We remember him.
At the blueness of the skies
and in the warmth of summer
At the rustling of the leaves
and in the beauty of autumn,
We remember him.
At the rising of the sun
and at its setting,
We remember him.
As long as we live, he too will live
For he is now a part of us,
As we remember him.

At every turning of my life
by Rabindranath Tagore

At every turning of my life
I came across
Good friends,
Friends who stood by me
Even when the time raced me by.
Farewell, farewell
My friends
I smile and
Bid you goodbye.
No, shed no tears
For I need them not
All I need is your smile.
If you feel sad
Do think of me
For that's what I'll like.
When you live in the hearts
Of those you love
Remember then
You never die

I Carry Your Heart by E.E. Cummings

I carry your heart with me (I carry it in my heart)
I am never without it
  (anywhere I go you go, my dear;
and whatever is done by only me
  is your doing, my darling)
I fear no fate (for you are my fate, my sweet)
I want no world (for beautiful
  you are my world, my true)
And it's you are whatever
  a moon has always meant
and whatever a sun will always sing is you
Here is the deepest secret
  nobody knows (here is the root of the root
and the bud of the bud
  and the sky of a tree called life;
which grows higher than soul
  can hope or mind can hide)
And this is the wonder
  that's keeping the stars apart
I carry your heart (I carry it in my heart)

If I should die by Christina Rossetti

If I should die and
Leave you here awhile
Be not like others sore undone,
Who keep long vigils
By the silent dust and weep.
For my sake turn again
To life and smile
Nerving thy heart
And trembling hand to do
Something to comfort
Other hearts than thine.
Complete these dear
Unfinished Tasks of mine,
And I, perchance
May therein comfort you.
Mary Lee Hall
When I am dead, my dearest,
Sing no sad songs for me;
Plant thou no roses at my head,
Nor shady cypress tree:
With showers and dewdrops wet;
And if thou wilt, remember,
And if thou wilt, forget..
I shall not see the shadows,
I shall not feel the rain;
I shall not hear the nightingale
Sing on, as if in pain;
And dreaming through the twilight

That doth not rise nor set,
Haply I may remember
And haply may forget.

Farewell, Sweet Dust by *Anonymous*

Now I have lost you, I must scatter
All of you on the air henceforth;
Not that to me it can ever matter
But it's only fair to the rest of the earth.
Now especially, when it is winter
And the sun's not half as bright as it was,
Who wouldn't be glad to find a splinter
That once was you, in the frozen grass?
Snowflakes, too, will be softer feathered,
Clouds, perhaps, will be whiter plumed;
Rain, whose brilliance you caught and gathered,
Purer silver have resumed.
Farewell, sweet dust; I never was a miser:
Once, for a minute, I made you mine:
Now you are gone, I am none the wiser
But the leaves of the willow are as bright as wine.

Turn Again To Life by Mary Lee Hall

If I should die and leave you here a while,
Be not like others sore undone,
Who keep long vigil by the silent dust.
For my sake turn again to life and smile,
Nerving thy heart and trembling hand to do
Something to comfort other hearts than thine.
Complete these dear unfinished tasks of mine
And I perchance may therein comfort you.

My candle burns at both ends
by Edna St.Vincent Millay

My candle burns at both ends;
It will not last the night;
But ah, my foes, and oh, my friends
It gives a lovely light!

He Is Gone by David Harkins.

You can shed tears that he is gone
Or you can smile because he has lived
You can close your eyes
and pray that he will come back
Or you can open your eyes
and see all that he has left
Your heart can be empty
because you can't see him
Or you can be full of the love that you shared
You can turn your back on tomorrow
and live yesterday
Or you can be happy for tomorrow
because of yesterday
You can remember him and only that he is gone
Or you can cherish his memory and let it live on
You can cry and close your mind,
be empty and turn your back
Or you can do what he would want:
   smile, open your eyes, love and go on.

Do not go gentle into that good night
by Dylan Thomas

Do not go gentle into that good night,
Old age should burn and rave at close of day;
Rage, rage against the dying of the light.

Though wise men at their end know dark is right,
Because their words had forked no lightning they
Do not go gentle into that good night.

Good men, the last wave by, crying how bright
Their frail deeds might have danced
  in a green bay,
Rage, rage against the dying of the light.

Wild men who caught and sang the sun in flight,
And learn, too late, they grieved it on its way,
Do not go gentle into that good night.

Grave men, near death, who see
  with blinding sight
Blind eyes could blaze like meteors and be gay,
Rage, rage against the dying of the light.

5 READINGS WITH FAITH

Parable On Immortality
by Henry Van Dyke

I am standing upon the seashore. A ship at my side spreads her white sails to the morning breeze and starts for the blue ocean. She is an object of beauty and strength. I stand and watch until at last she hangs like a speck of white cloud just where the sea and the sky come down to mingle with each other. Then someone at my side says, "There she goes."
Gone where? Gone from my sight...that is all. She is just as large in mast and hull and spar as she was when she left my side and just as able to bear her load of living freight to the place of destination. Her diminished size is in me, not in her. And just at the moment when someone at my side says, "There she goes", there are other eyes watching her coming and other voices ready to take up the glad shout, "Here she comes!"

Tis only we who grieve by *Anonymous*

Tis only we who grieve
They do not leave
They are not gone
They look upon us still
They walk among the valleys now
They stride upon the hill
Their smile is in the summer sky
Their grace is in the breeze
Their memories whisper in the grass
Their calm is in the trees
Their light is in the winter snow
Their tears are in the rain
Their merriment runs in the brook
Their laughter in the lane
Their gentleness is in the flowers
They sigh in autumn leaves
They do not leave
They are not gone
Tis only we who grieve
If only we could see the splendour of the land
To which our loved ones are called from you & me
We'd understand
If only we could hear the welcome they receive
From old familiar voices all so dear
We would not grieve
If only we could know the reason why they went
We'd smile and wipe away the tears that flow
And wait content.

Let Me Go by Christina Rossetti,

When I come to the end of the road
And the sun has set for me
I want no rites in a gloom filled room
Why cry for a soul set free?
Miss me a little, but not for long
And not with your head bowed low
Remember the love that once we shared
Miss me, but let me go.
For this is a journey we all must take
And each must go alone.
It's all part of the master plan
A step on the road to home.
When you are lonely and sick at heart
Go to the friends we know.
Laugh at all the things we used to do
Miss me, but let me go.

Death Is Nothing At All
by Canon Henry Scott-Holland

Death is nothing at all. I have only slipped away into the next room. I am I and you are you. Whatever we were to each other, that we are still. Call me by my old familiar name. Speak to me in the easy way you always used. Put no difference into your tone. Wear no forced air of solemnity or sorrow. Laugh as we always laughed at the little jokes we always enjoyed together.
Play, smile, think of me, pray for me. Let my name be ever the household word that it always was. Let it be spoken without effort, without the ghost of a shadow in it. Life means all that it ever meant. It is the same as it ever was.
There is absolute unbroken continuity.
What is death but a negligible accident?
Why should I be out of mind because I am out of sight? I am waiting for you for an interval. Somewhere very near, just around the corner.
All is well. Nothing is past; nothing is lost.
One brief moment, and all will be as it was before. How we shall laugh at the trouble of parting when we meet again!

You would know the secret of death
by Kahlil Gibran

"…You would know the secret of death.
But how shall you find it unless you seek it in the heart of life? The owl whose night-bound eyes are blind unto the day cannot unveil the mystery of light. If you would indeed behold the spirit of death, open your heart wide unto the body of life. For life and death are one, even as the river and the sea are one.
In the depth of your hopes and desires
lies your silent knowledge of the beyond; And like seeds dreaming beneath the snow, your heart dreams of spring. Trust the dreams, for in them is hidden the gate to eternity…
For what is it to die but to stand naked in the wind and to melt into the sun? And what is it to cease breathing, but to free the breath from its restless tides, that it may rise and expand and seek God unencumbered? Only when you drink from the river of silence shall you indeed sing. And when you have reached the mountain top, then you shall begin to climb. And when the earth shall claim your limbs, then shall you truly dance…"

We seem to give them back to Thee
by Bishop Brent

We seem to give them back to Thee, O God
   who gavest them to us.
Yet as Thou didst not lose them in giving,
So do we not lose them by their return.
Not as the world giveth,
   givest Thou O Lover of souls.
What Thou givest Thou takest not away,
For what is Thine is ours also if we are thine.
And life is eternal and love is immortal,
And death is only an horizon,
And an horizon is nothing
   save the limit of our sight.
Lift us up, strong Son of God
   that we may see further;
Cleanse our eyes that we may see more clearly;
Draw us closer to Thyself
That we may know ourselves to be nearer to our loved ones who are with Thee.
And while Thou dost prepare a place for us,
prepare us also for that happy place,
That where Thou art
   we may be also for evermore.

Irish Blessing by *Anonymous*

May the roads rise up to meet you.
May the wind be always at your back.
May the sun shine warm upon your face.
May the rains fall soft upon fields;
and until we meet again,
may God hold you in the palm of his hand.

6 BIBLE READINGS

John 14.1-6 "...In my Father's house there are many dwelling places..."

Let not your heart be troubled: ye believe in God, believe also in me. In my Father's house are many mansions: if it were not so, I would have told you. I go to prepare a place for you. And if I go and prepare a place for you, I will come again, and receive you unto myself; that where I am, there ye may be also. And whither I go ye know, and the way ye know. Thomas saith unto him, Lord, we know not whither thou goest; and how can we know the way? Jesus saith unto him,I am the way*, the truth, and the life: no man cometh unto the Father, but by me.

Psalm 23 "The Lord is my shepherd..."

The LORD is my shepherd; I shall not want.
He maketh me to lie down in green pastures:
he leadeth me beside the still waters.
He restoreth my soul:
he leadeth me in the paths of righteousness
 for his name's sake.
Yea, though I walk through the valley
 of the shadow of death,
I will fear no evil:
for thou art with me;
thy rod and thy staff they comfort me.
Thou preparest a table before me
in the presence of mine enemies:
thou anointest my head with oil;
my cup runneth over.
Surely goodness and mercy shall follow me
all the days of my life:
and I will dwell in the house of the LORD for ever.

Ecclesiastes 3 "…A time to every purpose…"

To every thing there is a season, and a time to
every purpose under the heaven:
A time to be born, and a time to die;
a time to plant, and a time to pluck up
that which is planted;
A time to kill, and a time to heal;
a time to break down, and a time to build up;
A time to weep, and a time to laugh;
a time to mourn, and a time to dance;
A time to cast away stones,
and a time to gather stones together;
a time to embrace,
and a time to refrain from embracing;
A time to get, and a time to lose;
a time to keep, and a time to cast away;
A time to rend, and a time to sew;
a time to keep silence, and a time to speak;
A time to love, and a time to hate;
a time of war, and a time of peace.
What profit hath he that worketh in that wherein
he laboureth? I have seen the travail, which God
hath given to the sons of men to be exercised in
it. He hath made every thing beautiful in his time:
also he hath set the world in their heart, so that
no man can find out the work that God maketh
from the beginning to the end.

Romans 8.35,37-39 "Who will separate us from the love of Christ?..."

Who shall separate us from the love of Christ?
Shall tribulation, or distress, or persecution, or famine, or nakedness, or peril, or sword?
Nay, in all these things we are more than conquerors through him that loved us.
For I am persuaded, that neither death, nor life, nor angels, nor principalities, nor powers, nor things present, nor things to come,
Nor height, nor depth, nor any other creature, shall be able to separate us from the love of God, which is in Christ Jesus our Lord.

Revelation 21.1-7 "I saw a new heaven and a new earth…"

And I saw a new heaven and a new earth: for the first heaven and the first earth were passed away; and there was no more sea. And I John saw the holy city, new Jerusalem, coming down from God out of heaven, prepared as a bride adorned for her husband. And I heard a great voice out of heaven saying, Behold, the tabernacle of God is with men, and he will dwell with them, and they shall be his people, and God himself shall be with them, and be their God. And God shall wipe away all tears from their eyes; and there shall be no more death, neither sorrow, nor crying, neither shall there be any more pain: for the former things are passed away. And he that sat upon the throne said, Behold, I make all things new. And he said unto me, Write: for these words are true and faithful. And he said unto me, It is done. I am Alpha and Omega, the beginning and the end. I will give unto him that is athirst of the fountain of the water of life freely. He that overcometh shall inherit all things; and I will be his God, and he shall be my son.

1 Corinthians 15.51-58 "…Where, O death, is your victory? Where, O death is your sting?…"

Behold, I shew you a mystery; We shall not all* sleep, but we shall all be changed, In a moment, in the twinkling of an eye, at the last trump: for the trumpet shall sound, and the dead shall be raised incorruptible, and we shall be changed. For this corruptible must put on incorruption, and this mortal must put on immortality. So when this corruptible shall have put on incorruption, and this mortal shall have put on immortality, then shall be brought to pass the saying that is written, Death is swallowed up in victory. O death, where is thy sting? O grave, where is thy victory? The sting of death is sin; and the strength of sin is the law. But thanks be to God, which giveth us the victory through our Lord Jesus Christ. Therefore, my beloved brethren, be ye stedfast, unmoveable, always abounding in the work of the Lord, forasmuch as ye know that your labour is not in vain in the Lord.

Psalm 121 "I lift up my eyes to the hills..."
I will lift up mine eyes unto the hills, from whence cometh my help. My help cometh from the LORD, which made heaven and earth. He will not suffer thy foot to be moved: he that keepeth thee will not slumber. Behold, he that keepeth Israel shall neither slumber nor sleep. The LORD is thy keeper: the LORD is thy shade upon thy right hand. The sun shall not smite thee by day, nor the moon by night. The LORD shall preserve thee from all evil: he shall preserve thy soul. The LORD shall preserve thy going out and thy coming in from this time forth, and even for evermore.

Wisdom 3.1-5,9 "...the souls of the righteous are in the hand of God..."

But the souls of the righteous
are in the hand of God,
and no torment will ever touch them.
In the eyes of the foolish
they seemed to have died,
and their departure was thought to be a disaster,
and their going from us to be their destruction;
but they are at peace.
For though in the sight of others
they were punished,
their hope is full of immortality.
Having been disciplined a little,
they will receive great good,
because God tested them
and found them worthy of himself;
Those who trust in him will understand truth,
and the faithful will abide with him in love,
because grace and mercy are upon his holy ones,
and he watches over his elect.

7 WRITING A EULOGY

This Chapter is aimed at those who want to write the eulogy themselves for a deceased loved one. Some people feel obliged to do deliver a eulogy, and it can be a meaningful last gift to give to someone. However, if you are not used to public speaking you may feel it is better to leave it to a celebrant or minister.

There is no right or wrong way to do this - some people want to do *something*, and some people just want to focus on their grief and leave the funeral in the hands of the celebrant.

Another option is to write the eulogy and give it to the celebrant to read out (it may help the flow if you can send an editable digital copy so the celebrant can put it into their own words). The 'last gift' can be just as meaningful if you prepare some words for someone else to read (and then all you have to do at he funeral is *mourn*).

A typical eulogy will start with a brief summary of the 'life story' of the deceased. This can include:

- Dates (the years) of birth, marriage(s), the start of jobs, births of children, retirement, significant deaths.
- Details of the chief mourners: husband/wife/partner, children, grandchildren, great grandchildren, parents, siblings, best friend...
- Where the deceased was born, brought up and

lived throughout their life.
- Schools, colleges, work places

All this information is important, it helps grieving families to take a *long view* of the life of the deceased: their loved one was more than the final few years of failing health. However, this biographical information is not the most important element of the eulogy. The most important thing is to capture the personality, what made him or her *tick*... So make sure to ask the family about the deceased's:

- Hobbies, interests and passions
- Achievements
- Personal qualities
- Philosophy of life / beliefs / faith

Make sure to include their love for the family (unless its one of those rare cases where the relationship was broken of negative).

The thought that maybe not everyone got on well with the deceased is something worth considering. Everyone present at the funeral will have their own view of the deceased: some may have found him/her to be generous, some may have found him/her to be cruel. A funeral is not the place to list someone's faults, but it is also important to tactfully acknowledge if there were issues. Phrases like, "you will be aware that he was not perfect," or "she was not always the easiest person to get along with," can be useful in these circumstances.

One phrase I often use (even when I don't pick up on family discord) is "you may remember..." I would list the qualities I have been told about the deceased like this:

"You may remember his love of his family..."

"You may remember her passion for discussing politics..."

"You may remember his enthusiasm for helping with family D.I.Y. projects..."

"You may remember her enjoyment of her motorbike..."

The use of the work "may" allows for other people with other memories to feel that their view can also be legitimate.

Finally, if you are a celebrant taking a service for someone you haven't met, always tell the congregation. A phrase I often use in these circumstances is "Sadly, I did not have the privilege of meeting [*Name*] during *his/her* life, but you will have many memories..." This humility places the focus on the memories of those who mourn and diffuses any potential for people to wonder 'who do they think they are?' or simply to wonder 'how do they know the deceased?'

8 SYMBOLIC ACTS

One thing religious worship does well is symbolism. Sometimes words do not seem to be enough, so sharing a cup of wine, sprinkling some water, lighting a candle or burning incense can add a focus, depth and profundity to a gathering. In this next section I will consider the 'pros' and 'cons' of some of the most common Symbolic Acts that can be done before, during or after a funeral:

Releasing Doves

This can be beautiful and uplifting, but you shouldn't consider it unless you have a sense of humour! If you want to release a dove or doves you will need a willingness to accept that it may not go quite as planned. Doves are wild animals, and do not always soar majestically into the sky. I have seen them refuse to leave their box, and have heard of a funeral where one flew straight in through the window of the crematorium toilet! (I also heard of a more tragic event where one flew straight under the wheels of a passing car!)

Releasing Balloons

Balloons with messages for the deceased or a prayer are more reliable than doves, but still have their problems: make sure they are filled with helium rather than just blown up (this seems

obvious, but grieving families are not always able to do their best thinking when overcome with sadness).
Strong wind may cause problems. Also there are environmental concerns with both the use of helium and the litter caused when the balloon eventually returns to earth.

Sprinkling Water

There is a Christian tradition of sprinkling the coffin with holy water. Water is used to mark the beginning of life in baptism, it can be used at a funeral as a symbol of symmetry; or if the family have faith the water can be seen as marking the new life the deceased is embarking on in God's eternal kingdom.

Taking Stones

Stones can be used in lots of ways: given as people enter to be placed at the foot of the coffin, or taken away to be placed in gardens / plant pots (if you announce that people are to take them, don't assume everyone has a garden!)
As an alternative to stones people could be given autumn leaves to meditate on.
Stones work particularly well at a burial. Don't have them dropped onto the coffin (unless they are very small they could damage the coffin, and will make a horrible hollow crashing noise!) but they could be left in a pile at the head of the

grave like a cairn.

Taking Ashes

This is an idea that I would like for my own funeral, and one that I haven't seen done elsewhere. I would like to be cremated directly and without ceremony (this is significantly cheaper than a full funeral) and then my ashes brought to a Church of Community Hall for a memorial Service. At the end of the service everyone would be given a small biodegradable box of my ashes to take and bury or scatter somewhere beautiful. I want to return to nature as soon as possible and be back in the circle of nature...

A Book of Remembrance

A book of remembrance is a lovely thing to have, but here are a few pointers to organising one: The average attendance at a funeral is probably around twenty, so don't buy a book of five hundred pages, or it will look very empty. In fact it is probably best to work with loose pages that you can have bound after the event. That has several advantages: firstly, it can have as many pages as you require; secondly, several people can write their comments at the same time rather than being crowded around one book; thirdly, people that couldn't make the funeral due to distance or ill-health can send pages...

Lighting Candles

I am very fond of candles, the flickering of a dozen or more tiny lights can be very evocative. However health and safety policies often make this impossible. Also to do it safely you need a proper stand, or at least a large tray of sand, and many venues are justifiably squeamish about the mess sand and hot wax can create as well as the risk of fire. Check with the venue before offering this to the family.

Carrying the Coffin

Tell the funeral director in advance, he or she will leave a little time to run through how to do the lifting safely and with dignity. However, even if you are pretty certain that you will want to carry the coffin I would advise you to tell the funeral director that you will decide depending on how you feel on the day. That way the funeral director will still provide bearers.

At a burial I would strongly advise against the family lowering the coffin into the grave. This is a lot more difficult than it looks, I have never seen it done with the coffin lowered evenly and without at least one of the family ending up with serious rope burns.

Jewellery made from ashes

This is offered by some funeral directors or other companies (you can even have ashes placed in a sex toy!)
There is no right or wrong approach, but I would suggest having a look at an example of the work before ordering. It would be a shame to have your mother/brother/sister/son immortalised in something that looks naff. (Early attempts to turn human ashes into diamonds created stones with an unpleasant yellowish colour - but the technology is improving all the time.)

A word about ashes:

You have said goodbye you do not *need* a further ritual. A further ritual may be helpful, but it is not necessary.
I would ask you to consider allowing the crematorium to respectfully scatter them in their memorial garden. I have worked for a funeral director where there was a room full of ashes that families could not bring themselves to collect, so they they were left on the shelf for years, sometimes decades.
A respectful scattering by crematorium staff is better than spending years in a dusty, dark room.

9 CELEBRATING A LIFE OR MOURNING A DEATH?

Organising a funeral is a balancing act. Often families don't want it to be too sad, preferring a celebration. This is well-meaning and people have a right to choose how they organise the funeral of their loved ones. However, they also have a psychological need to mourn. Therefore (unless I am explicitly told not to do it) I *always* allow for a moment of silence and a moment to say goodbye. I have created this pause for sadness in even the most joyful celebrations and I have never once had a complaint about it, but rather have had literally hundreds of people tell me that it was "just right."

Nobody *wants* to be sad, but when someone we love dies we need to experience sadness or we are storing up problems for the future.

I like the approach to funerals that sees them as a celebration, but we must also allow room for mourning or we are short-changing the bereaved. I always feel pleased at a funeral where the family were comfortable enough to laugh at funny memories and cry for their loss.

10 ABOUT THE AUTHOR

I was born in Belfast, moved to London for University via a year in Zimbabwe (I never had a great sense of direction). I was a Vicar for many years, and a Prison Chaplain, before becoming a Funeral Arranger in North London. I now work as a freelance Funeral Celebrant while volunteering for Cruse Bereavement Care and Eleanor Hospice. I am also training to be a Counsellor. (I think I must hate free time!)

I have written four books: the Wild Strawberry Trilogy and The Parliament of the Dead, this is my first work of non-fiction.

My partner, Sandi, keeps me sane, without her love and support so much time in the land of the dead would get too much...

Printed in Great Britain
by Amazon